Usborne Beginners

Sun, Moon and stars

Stephanie Turnbull
Designed by Zöe Wray

Illustrated by Kuo Kang Chen and Uwe Mayer

Space consultant: Stuart Atkinson

Reading consultant: Alison Kelly,
University of Surrey Roehampton

SCHOLASTIC INC.

New York Toronto London Auckland Sydney
Mexico City New Delhi Hong Kong Buenos Aires

Contents

The night sky

When you look at the night sky, you can see shining stars, far away in space.

You might be able to spot the Moon too.

Everything you can see is only a tiny part of space.

The Moon looks small, but it would take about four days to drive all the way around it.

Out in space

Our planet Earth is a lump of rock in space. It is one of a group of nine planets.

Each planet goes around the Sun on its own invisible path.

The Sun and the planets are called the Solar System.

Sun

Mercury

Venus

Earth

Mars

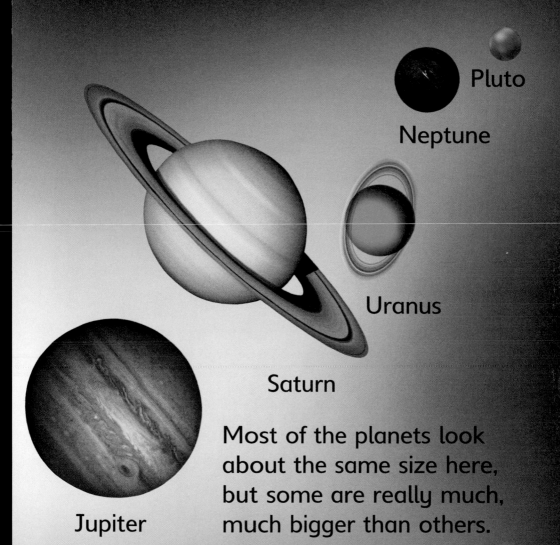

Pluto

Neptune

Uranus

Saturn

Jupiter

Most of the planets look about the same size here, but some are really much, much bigger than others.

Pluto is so far away from Earth that a fast spacecraft would take ten years to get there.

The Sun

The Sun is a star. It is the closest star to Earth, so it looks bigger than other stars.

The Sun was formed by thick clouds of dust and gas.

It became a glowing ball of gas that is hottest in the middle.

The surface of the Sun bubbles and boils.

Sunspot

The Sun has dark areas called sunspots.
They are cooler than the rest of the Sun.

Never look straight
at the Sun. Its
strong light can
hurt your eyes.

Earth and Sun

Earth turns as it moves around the Sun.

The parts of Earth facing the Sun have day.
Parts that light doesn't reach have night. As
Earth turns, different parts have day or night.

When it gets dark where you
live, it is just getting light on
the other side of Earth.

The Sun is a long way away from Earth. A spacecraft called Ulysses studies the Sun from space.

It can't fly too close to the Sun, because it would melt in the heat.

The Sun gives us light and heat. No plants or animals could live without it.

Nearby planets

The four planets closest to the Sun are Mercury, Venus, Earth and Mars.

They are all rocky planets, but Earth is the only one that plants and animals live on.

This is Venus. It has high mountains and volcanoes. The planet's air is poisonous.

A few years ago, a small spacecraft was sent to Mars.

The spacecraft opened up and a robot car drove out.

The car was about the size of a skateboard. Scientists on Earth used computers to make it move and take photos.

Mercury is so close to the Sun that the land is hotter than boiling water.

Faraway planets

Jupiter, Saturn, Uranus, Neptune and Pluto are far away from the Sun. They are very cold places.

Jupiter is the biggest planet in the Solar System.

This red spot on Jupiter is a storm that is about twice the size of Earth.

Saturn has bright rings around it.

From far away, Saturn's rings look like solid hoops.

In fact each ring is made up of dust, rocks and ice.

The surface of Pluto is frozen, like a huge skating rink.

The Moon

The Moon is a ball of rock that goes around and around the Earth.

As the Moon moves, the Sun lights up different parts of it. This is why the Moon seems to change shape in the night sky.

When the Sun shines
behind the Moon, you
can't see its light side.
It is called a New Moon.

Sometimes you can
only see part of the
Moon. This is called
a Crescent Moon.

When the Sun lights
up the whole side
of the Moon, you
can see a Full Moon.

Other planets have moons too.
Jupiter has more than 40 moons.

A rocky desert

The Moon is a dry, dusty place. It has no air or water, so nothing lives there.

The Moon's surface is rocky and hilly. It is covered in giant holes called craters.

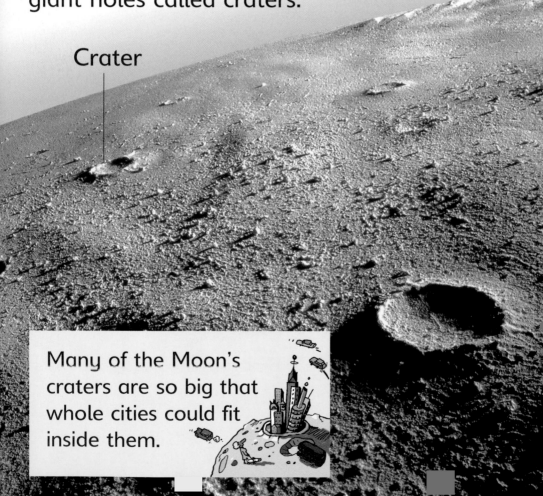

Crater

Many of the Moon's craters are so big that whole cities could fit inside them.

There are lots of rocks
drifting in space.

Sometimes a rock crashes
into the Moon.

The rock explodes and dust
flies everywhere.

It makes a deep,
bowl-shaped crater.

Moon missions

The Moon is the only place in space where people have landed. This is how astronauts got there.

1. A rocket blasted off into space, with astronauts inside.

2. Parts of the rocket fell away, leaving a small spacecraft.

3. A lunar module came out and landed on the Moon.

4. Astronauts climbed down the ladder onto the Moon's surface.

Astronauts explored the Moon in an electric car. They collected rocks to bring back.

This is a piece of rock from the Moon.

In the future, scientists might build special hotels on the Moon for people to stay in.

Vanishing trick

Sometimes the Moon moves in front
of the Sun and blocks out the Sun's light.
This is called a solar eclipse.

This black circle is the
Moon, covering the Sun.
Gases from the Sun
glow around the edges.

At the start of an eclipse, the Sun looks
as if it has a bite taken out of it.

As the Moon covers more of the Sun,
the sky gets darker and it feels colder.

The Moon covers the Sun completely
for a short time.

During an eclipse,
many animals think it must
be night, so they get ready to sleep.

Stars

Stars are glowing balls of gas, like the Sun.

The bright star in this photo is much bigger than the Sun, but it looks small because it is so far away.

Some stars slowly get bigger and duller over many years.

They puff off layers of gas and slowly fade away.

Many stars move around in pairs. They are called double stars.

Some big stars explode. This cloud of gas is all that's left of an exploded star.

Star groups

Stars can be joined up
to make patterns.

This pattern of stars is
called the Great Dog.

If lines join the stars, you
can see a dog shape.

A group of billions of stars is called
a galaxy. One galaxy is called the
Whirlpool because of its swirling shape.

The Whirlpool galaxy

Most galaxies are spiral or oval shapes. One galaxy looks like a wheel.

Shooting stars

A shooting star is not really a star.
It is a small, hot piece of space rock.

Shooting stars are also
known as meteors.
They look like stars
falling out of the sky.

Often lots of space
rocks fall at once.
This is called a
meteor shower.

Space rocks heat up if they come too near Earth.

They burn away, leaving a trail of light behind them.

Some rocks are too big to burn up, so they hit Earth. This huge crater was made by a rock that fell in Arizona, U.S.A.

Space watch

People use telescopes to look at space.
They make things look bigger and clearer.

This huge telescope floats around Earth.
It takes photos and sends them back to Earth.

A spacecraft took the
telescope into space.

A robot arm lifted
the telescope out.

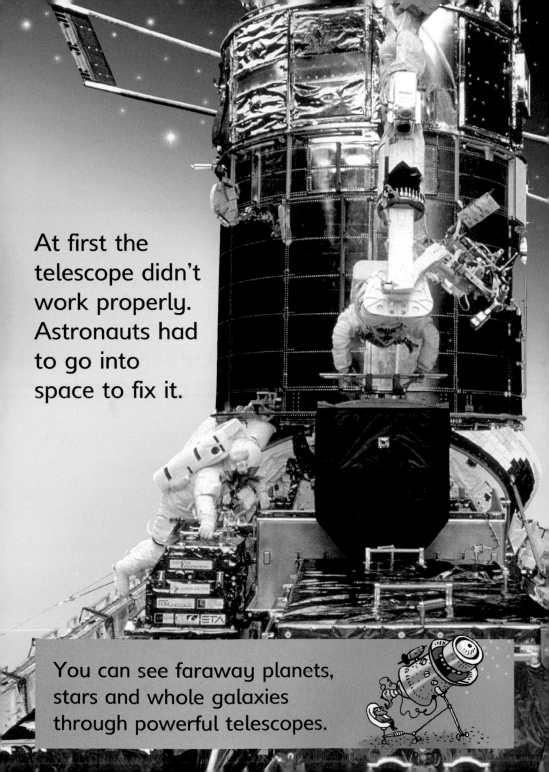

At first the telescope didn't work properly. Astronauts had to go into space to fix it.

You can see faraway planets, stars and whole galaxies through powerful telescopes.

Glossary of space words

Here are some of the words in this book you might not know. This page tells you what they mean.

 planet - a huge round object in space. Earth is a planet.

 Solar System - the Sun and the nine planets that go around it.

 crater - a hole on the Moon or a planet, made by a space rock hitting it.

 astronaut - a person who is specially trained to travel into space.

 lunar module - a small spacecraft that landed on the Moon.

 galaxy - a group of billions of stars. There are millions of galaxies in space.

 telescope - something that makes things far away look bigger and closer.

Websites to visit

If you have a computer, you can find out more about the Sun, Moon and stars on the Internet. On the Usborne Quicklinks website there are links to four fun websites.

Website 1 - Help a spaceship find its way through a space maze.

Website 2 - Try to match the pairs of space pictures.

Website 3 - Shade in a space picture.

Website 4 - Join the dots to make different star patterns.

To visit these websites, go to **www.usborne-quicklinks.com** and type the keywords "beginners sun". Then click on the link for the website you want to visit. Before you use the Internet, look at the safety guidelines inside the back cover of this book and ask an adult to read them with you.

Index

Acknowledgements

Managing editor: Fiona Watt, Managing designer: Mary Cartwright
Cover design: Nicola Butler
Photographic manipulation by Emma Julings and John Russell

Photo credits

The publishers are grateful to the following for permission to reproduce material:
© **Alamy** 2-3 (Doug Steley), 16 (Pictor International), 20 (Novastock); © **Corbis** 1
(Myron Jay Dorf), 8 (Roger Ressmeyer), 27 (Charles & Josette Lenars); © **David A. Hardy** 9;
© **Digital Vision** Cover (Earth); © **ESO/NASA** 22-23, 24-25, 30 (galaxy); © **NASA**
Cover (Moon), 4-5, 6-7, 14, 15, 19, 28, 29, 31; © **Science Photo Library** 10
(David P. Anderson, SMU/NASA), 11 & 12 (NASA), 13

Every effort has been made to trace and acknowledge ownership of copyright. If any rights have
been omitted, the publishers offer to rectify this in any subsequent editions following notification.